MW01675423

پرسکون نیند سو جاؤ، ننھے بھیڑئیے

Dors bien, petit loup

Ulrich Renz · Barbara Brinkmann

پرسکون نیند سو جاؤ، ننھے بھیڑئیے

Dors bien, petit loup

ترجمہ:

Muhammad Yahya, Dr. Laila Mushfa (اردو)

Céleste Lottigier (فرانسیسی)

sefa

آڈیو بوک اور ویڈیو:

www.sefa-bilingual.com/bonus

مفت رسائی کے لیے پاس ورڈ:

اردو: **Sorry, audio or video is not yet available in this language.**

فرانسیسی: **LWFR1527**

We are currently working on making as many of our bilingual books as possible available to you as audio books and videos. We kindly ask for your patience if there is no audio or video version in your language yet! You can keep up with the progress of our work on our website:
www.sefa-bilingual.com/languages

شب بخیر، ٹم! ہم کل اپنی تلاش جاری رکھیں گے۔
اب سکون سے سو جائو۔

Bonne nuit, Tim ! On continuera à chercher demain.
Dors bien maintenant !

باہر پہلے ہی اندھیرا ہو گیا ہے۔

Dehors, il fait déjà nuit.

ٹم کیا کر رہا ہے؟

Mais que fait Tim là ?

وہ کھیل کے میدان میں جانے کے لیئے نکل رہا ہے۔
وہ یہاں کیا تلاش کر رہا ہے؟

Il va dehors, à l’aire de jeu.

Qu’est-ce qu’il y cherche ?

ننھے بھیڑئیے!

وہ اس کے بغیر نہیں سو سکتا۔

Le petit loup !

Sans lui, il ne peut pas dormir.

یہ کون آ رہا ہے؟

Mais qui arrive là ?

میری! وہ اپنی گیند تلاش کر رہی ہے۔

Marie ! Elle cherche son ballon.

اور ٹوبی کیا ڈھونڈ رہا ہے؟

Et Tobi, qu’est-ce qu’il cherche ?

اپنا کھدائی کرنے والا آلہ۔

Sa pelleteuse.

اور نالا کیا ڈھونڈ رہی ہے؟

Et Nala, qu’est-ce qu’elle cherche ?

اپنی گڑیا۔

Sa poupée.

کیا بچوں کو بستر پہ نہیں جانا ہے؟
بلی بہت زیادہ حیران ہوئی۔

Les enfants ne doivent-ils pas aller au lit ?

Le chat est très surpris.

7
vitrerie
chez Mastin

اب کون آ رہا ہے؟

Qui vient donc là ?

ٹم کے امی اور ابو!
وہ اپنے ٹم کے بغیر نہیں سو سکتے۔

Le papa et la maman de Tim !
Sans leur Tim, ils ne peuvent pas dormir.

ان میں سےزیادہ تر لوگ آ رہے ہیں!
میری کے ابو، ٹوبی کے دادا اور نالا کی امی۔

Et en voilà encore d'autres qui arrivent !
Le papa de Marie. Le papi de Tobi. Et la maman de Nala.

اب جلدی بستر پہ جائو!

Vite au lit maintenant !

شب بخیر، ٹم! کل ہمیں مزید تلاش نہیں کرنا ہوگا۔

Bonne nuit, Tim !

Demain nous n’aurons plus besoin de chercher.

پرسکون نیند سو جاؤ، ننھے بھیڑئیے!

Dors bien, petit loup !

مصنفين

Ulrich Renz was born in Stuttgart, Germany, in 1960. After studying French literature in Paris he graduated from medical school in Lübeck and worked as head of a scientific publishing company. He is now a writer of non-fiction books as well as children's fiction books.

www.ulrichrenz.de

Barbara Brinkmann was born in Munich in 1969 and grew up in the foothills of the Bavarian Alps. She studied architecture in Munich and is currently a research associate in the Department of Architecture at the Technical University of Munich. She also works as a freelance graphic designer, illustrator, and author.

www.bcbrinkmann.de

Do you like drawing?

Here are the pictures from the story to color in:

www.sefa-bilingual.com/coloring

Enjoy!

جنگلی ہنس

مأخوذة عن قصة لهانز كريستيان اندرسن

► Recommended age: 4-5 and up

ہینس کرسٹن اینڈرسن کی کہانی جنگلی ہنس، دنیا کی مشہور ترین بامقصد پریوں کی کہانیوں میں سے ایک ہے۔ یہ کہانی انسانی ڈرامہ کے ہر موضوع ؛ خوف، بہادری، محبت، دھوکہ، جدائی، اور ملن کا بہت خوبصورتی سے احاطہ کرتی ہے۔

Available in your language?

► Check out with our „Language Wizard":

www.sefa-bilingual.com/languages

My Most Beautiful Dream

► Reading age: 2-3 and up

Lulu can't fall asleep. All her cuddly toys are dreaming already – the shark, the elephant, the little mouse, the dragon, the kangaroo, and the lion cub. Even the bear has trouble keeping his eyes open...
Hey bear, will you take me along into your dream?
Thus begins a journey for Lulu that leads her through the dreams of her cuddly toys – and finally to her own most beautiful dream.

Available in your language?

► Check out with our „Language Wizard":

www.sefa-bilingual.com/languages

© 2023 by Sefa Verlag Kirsten Bödeker, Lübeck, Germany

www.sefa-verlag.de

IT: Paul Bödeker, Freiburg, Germany

Font: Noto Sans

All rights reserved. No part of this book may be reproduced without the written consent of the publisher

ISBN: 9783739919119

CPSIA information can be obtained
at www.ICGtesting.com
Printed in the USA
LVHW070729040423
743407LV00008B/196

9 783739 919119